COMPOSER
SHOWCASE
HAL LEONARD
STUDENT PIANO LIBRARY

T0055812

Alaska Sketches

EIGHT PIECES FOR PIANO SOLO

BY LYNDA LYBECK-ROBINSON

CONTENTS

2 *Performance Notes*

4 Aurora Borealis

8 Gold Miner's Lullaby

12 Hungry Sea

16 Iditarod

26 Raven Play

30 Russian Holiday

21 Summer Bay Love

34 Williwaw

ISBN 978-1-4803-4433-4

HAL•LEONARD®
CORPORATION
7777 W. BLUEMOUND RD. P.O. BOX 13819 MILWAUKEE, WI 53213

In Australia Contact:
Hal Leonard Australia Pty. Ltd.
4 Lentara Court
Cheltenham, Victoria, 3192 Australia
Email: ausadmin@halleonard.com.au

Visit Hal Leonard Online at
www.halleonard.com

Performance Notes

The beauty and mystique of Alaska provide inspiration for composers, artists, and authors of all ages. *Alaska Sketches* was composed in the small, remote Aleutian Island community of Unalaska, known best for its fishing industry and stunning backdrop. This island chain reaches out from Alaska's western coast toward Russia, surrounded by the Bering Sea's splendor and power. *Alaska Sketches* is a beautiful sampling of the enormous cache of revelations that all of Alaska, "the last frontier," has to offer.

Williwaw

A williwaw is a sudden violent squall blowing offshore from a mountainous coast. In the Bering Sea's Aleutian Islands, a williwaw is used to describe the funnels of spray that whip upward from the whitecaps in a violent wind. The intensity of the eighth note interplay between the right and left hands starts this piece off with passionate appeal. While playing this piece, pianists may imagine the rising and falling of the furious wind gusts. Note the pianistic patterns and simple chord changes throughout that make this piece accessible while still sounding impressive and difficult.

Iditarod

The annual Iditarod sled dog race runs from the streets of Anchorage to Nome, Alaska in the far north, capturing the attention and excitement of residents and fans around the world. The initial repeating left-hand pattern imitates the steady insistent pace of the team of huskies, urged on by the snap of the whip cracking through the icy air, spurring the dogs forward in this joyful and energetic piece.

Summer Bay Love

Your kayak lies tilted on the shore in the lapping waves while the bonfire of driftwood crackles. Hungry from the day's journey, you rest and share an evening picnic with someone special. The sound of a splash is carried over the breeze, and you look in time to see humpbacks blowing, breaching and sounding in the bay just as the sun sets in the west. *Summer Bay Love* is a classical/romantic/pop style piece, featuring a lovely melody weaving over left-hand arpeggios.

Hungry Sea

This piece is powerful, dangerous, and mighty! The left hand crossing over the right hand represents the unpredictable pounding and rolling of the sea in a typical Bering Sea storm, punctuated by moments of dissonance and resolution. Though the piece moves quickly, pedal lightly, be aware of the melody, and keep your life jacket handy.

Gold Miner's Lullaby

The Gold Rush of the 1890s attracted fortune seekers from around the world and created an economic foundation for the prosperous group of pioneers who built what was to become the state of Alaska in 1959. The romance of their quest remains today. *Gold Miner's Lullaby* is a waltz reminiscent of an early 20th century American ballad. The melody is wistful, yet warm, lonely, and yet romantic enough for a dance by candlelight.

Russian Holiday

Early Russian explorers laid down their mark on the Alaskan wilderness and its people. The Russian Orthodox churches and colorful cupolas are a familiar symbol of their rich culture past and present. Keep the pedal light while enjoying the traditional flavor of this Russian dance in A minor.

Raven Play

Talons clutched in mid air with wings flapping, the playful dance of ravens is both fascinating and delightful. The motive of this piece begins with hands intertwined on intervals of a 5th, quickly, deftly dancing from one octave to another. Left hand crosses over the right, as the birds dodge and tease one another in real life. The key to success in this piece is discovering the patterns that will make the piece easier to play than at first glance.

Aurora Borealis

Bright, dancing, eerie, weaving neon colors on a black sky peppered with stars, make you draw in a breath of icy winter air. To create these northern lights in sound, keep the pedal steady but take care to draw out the lovely melody. This will create a freehand musical sketch portraying a mesmerizing show of electrically charged particles from the sun as they enter the earth's atmosphere.

Alaska Sketches may be played with a certain amount of your own interpretive passion. The solos were written as I "saw" them, and, as in the *Raven Play* and *Hungry Sea*, left-hand crossings become very familiar to the player, and are as theatrical as the subjects are in person. Tempo markings don't need to be exact, however, keep in mind that a *Williwaw's* sea spray, spinning in a furious wind across the surface of the sea, cannot happen slowly and a *Summer Bay Love* would not be a mood one would rush.

Alaska Sketches is dedicated to my students that delight and motivate me every day. I'm especially grateful to my generous friends and colleagues Ann Fernandez and Jean Hinkle who have played through these from the start and shared their (and their students') feedback over the Internet from thousands of miles away. I'm fortunate to have known many extraordinary teachers in my own education, but it was Dr. Jill Timmons at Linfield College whose influence moved me to ultimately make music education my life, so many thanks to Dr. Timmons! Finally, I offer my heartfelt appreciation to composer, pedagogue, editor, and friend Jennifer Linn, who loves Alaska, and, from even before our first meeting, has been a great inspiration to me.

—Lynda Lybeck-Robinson

Aurora Borealis

By Lynda Lybeck-Robinson

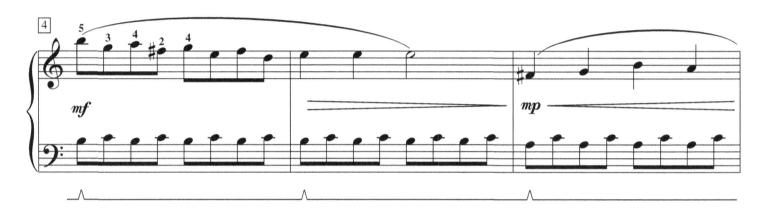

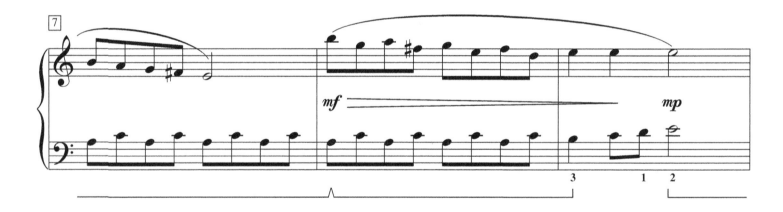

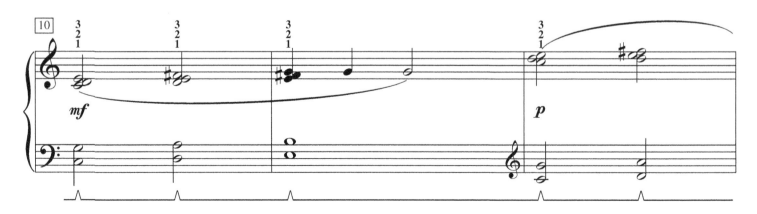

Gold Miner's Lullaby

*For Amirelle, with love, *Tetushka ("Tuutka-x")*

By Lynda Lybeck-Robinson

Tetushka means Auntie in Russian, Tuutka-x is Auntie in Unangan, the indiginous language of the Aleut people.

Hungry Sea

By Lynda Lybeck-Robinson

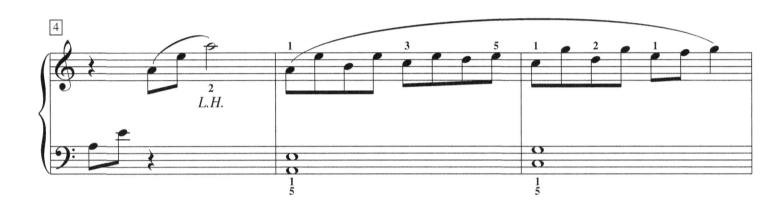

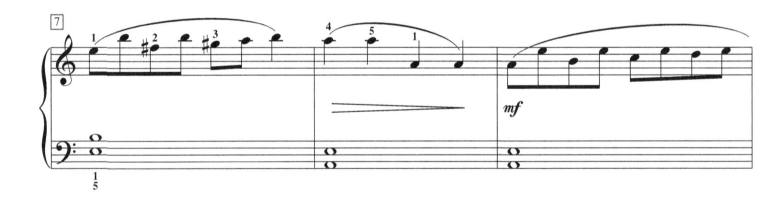

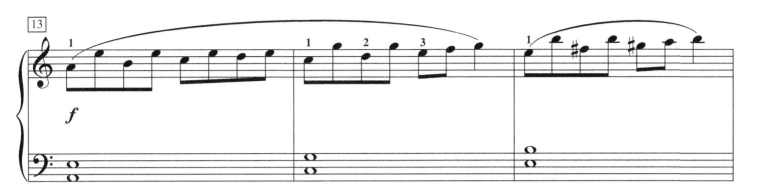

19 Suspenseful

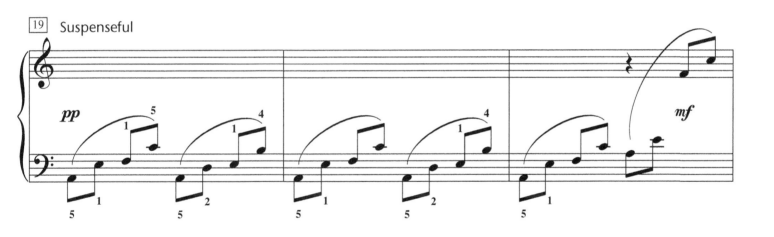

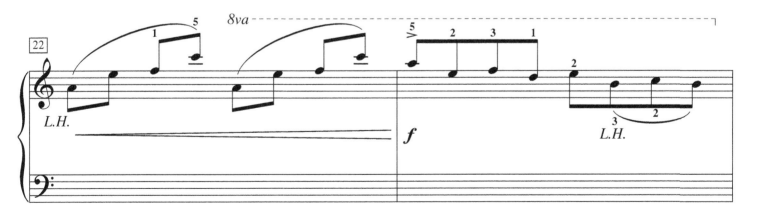

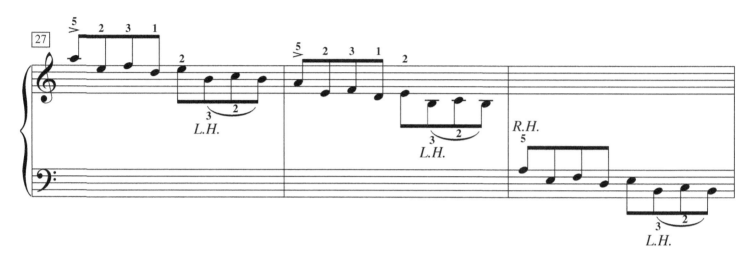

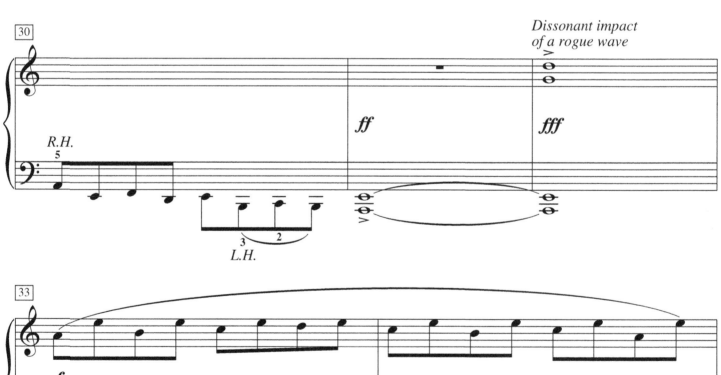

Dissonant impact of a rogue wave

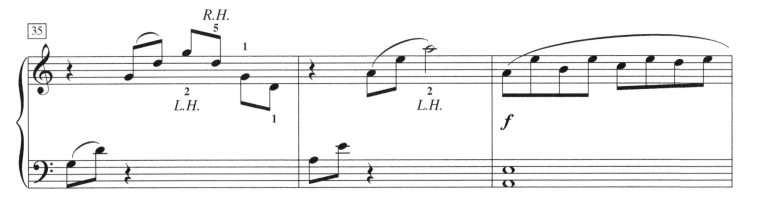

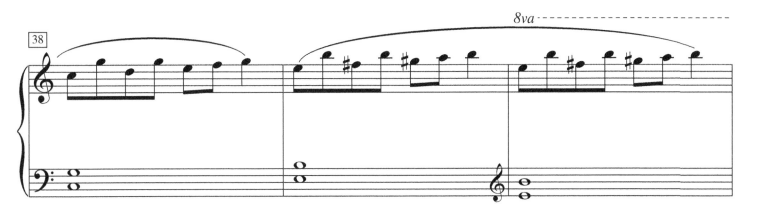

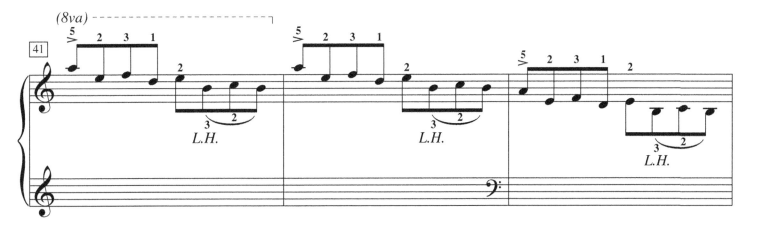

Iditarod

By Lynda Lybeck-Robinson

With intensity (♩ = 176)

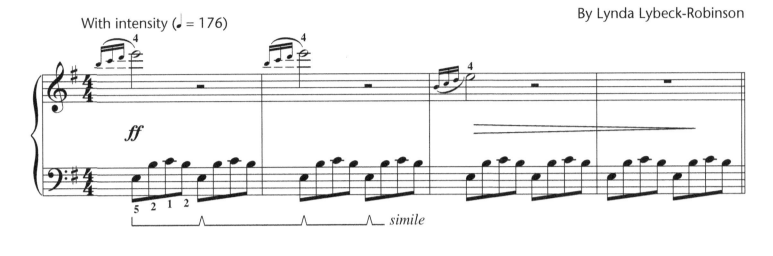

R.H. 8va on repeat

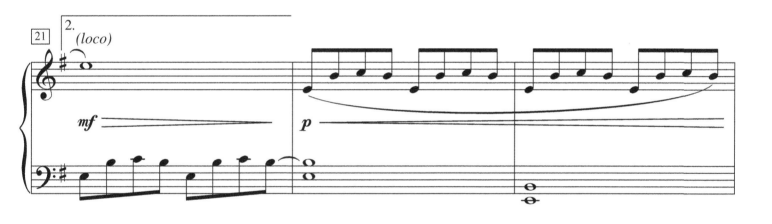

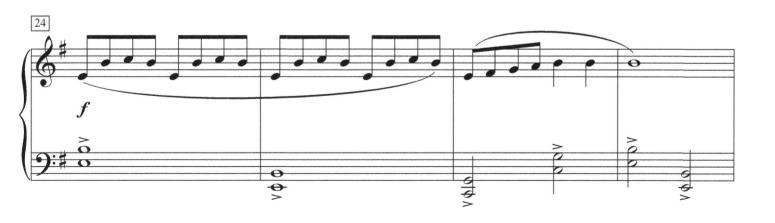

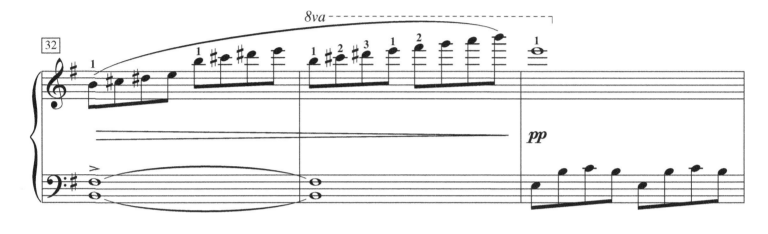

Summer Bay Love

For Mia

By Lynda Lybeck-Robinson

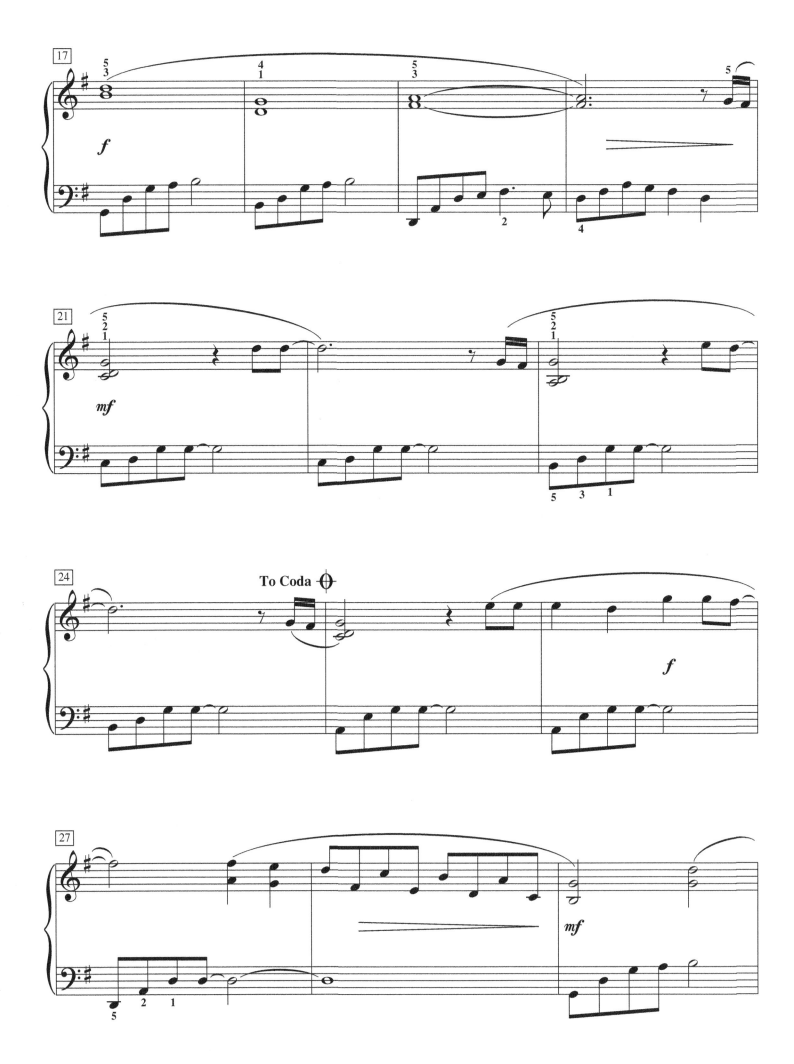

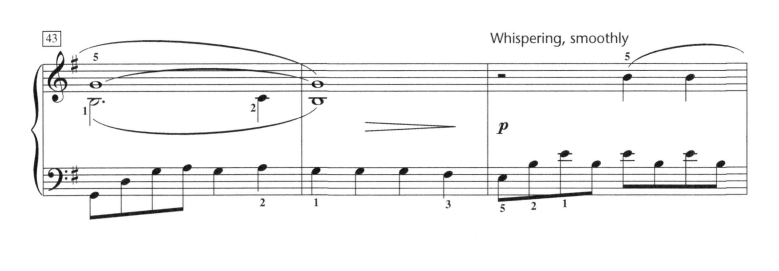

Whispering, smoothly

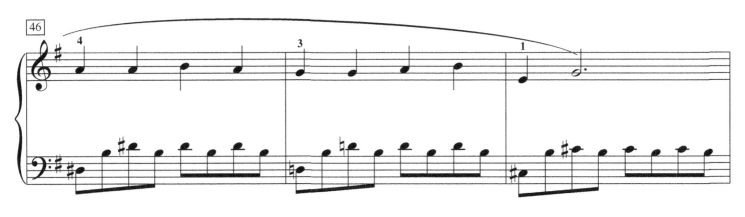

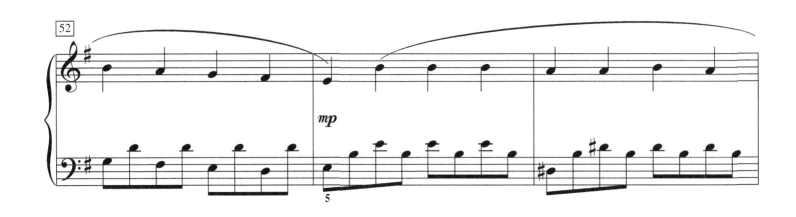

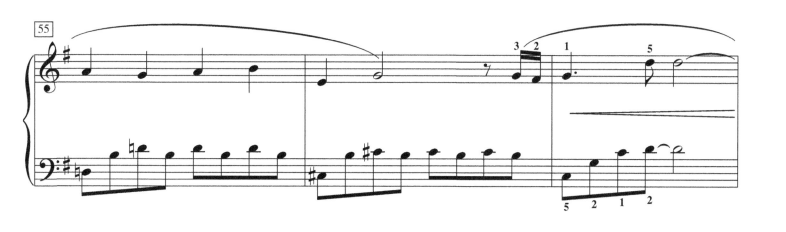

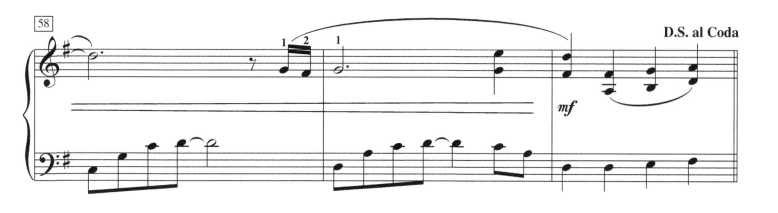

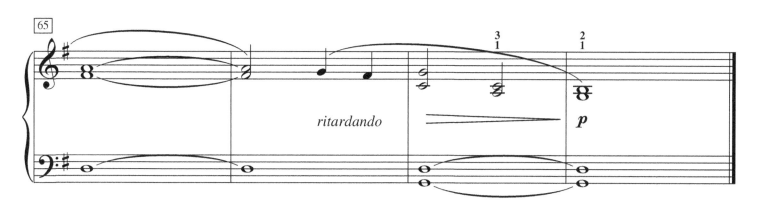

Raven Play

By Lynda Lybeck-Robinson

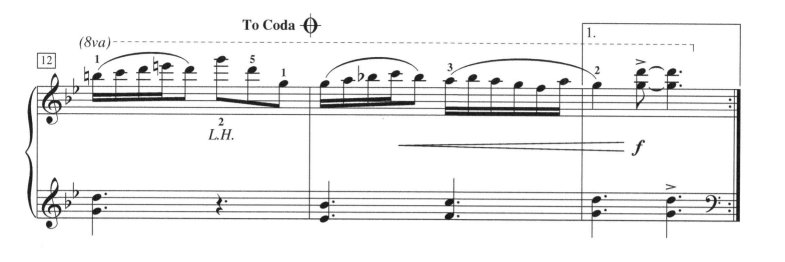

Left hand boldly crosses over right hand as if choreographing a "raven dance."

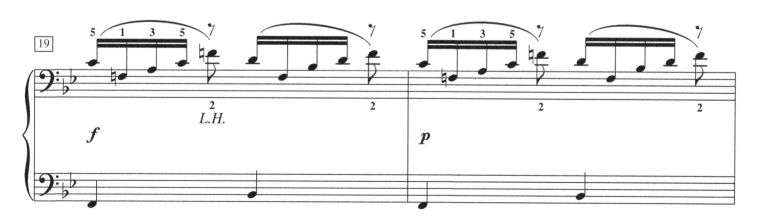

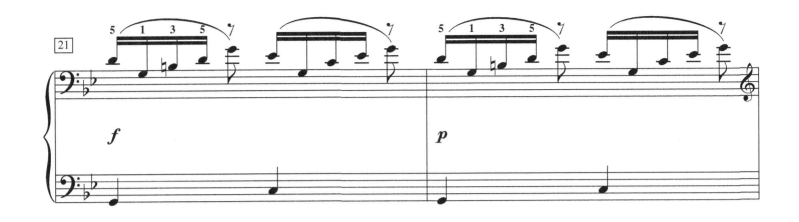

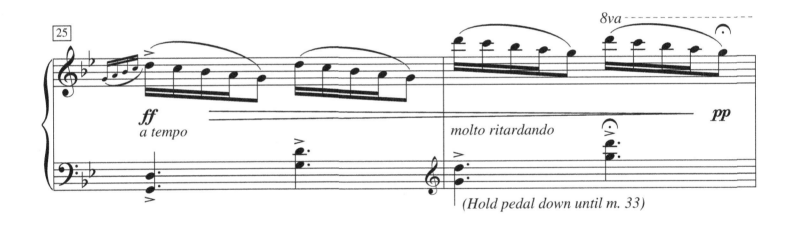

(Hold pedal down until m. 33)

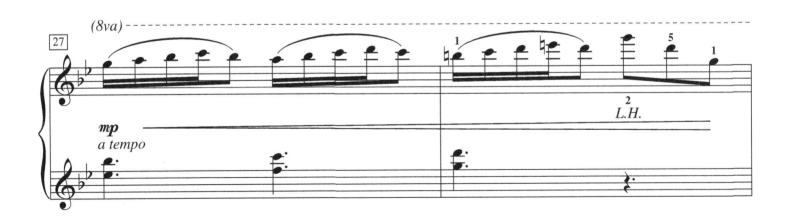

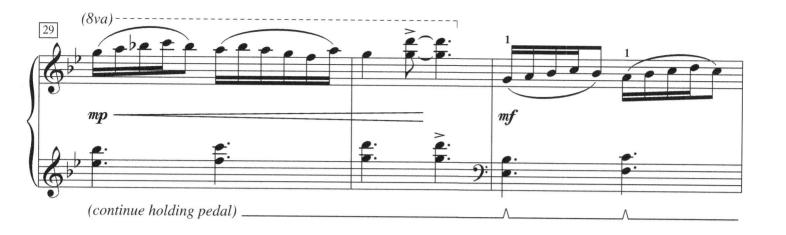

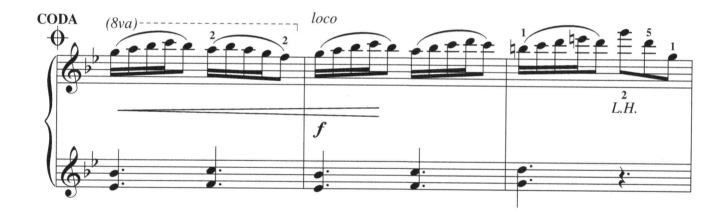

Russian Holiday

By Lynda Lybeck-Robinson

With hushed intensity

ff   *pp*

mp

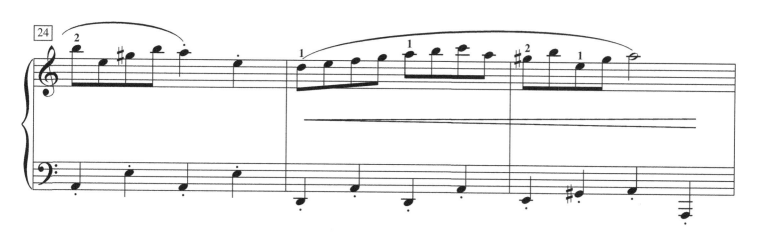

Williwaw

For Daniel

By Lynda Lybeck-Robinson

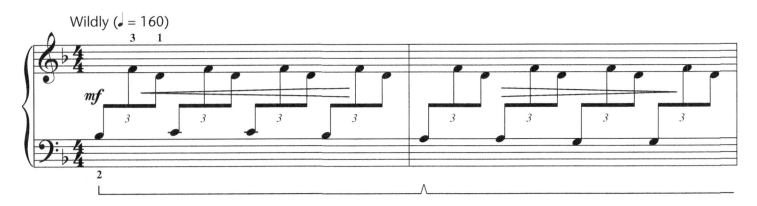

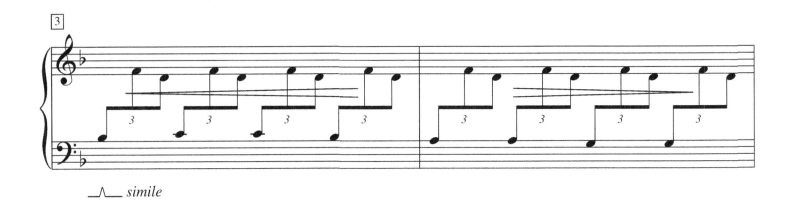

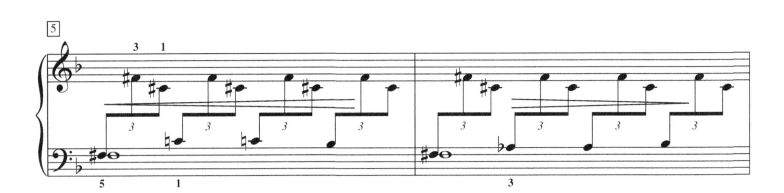

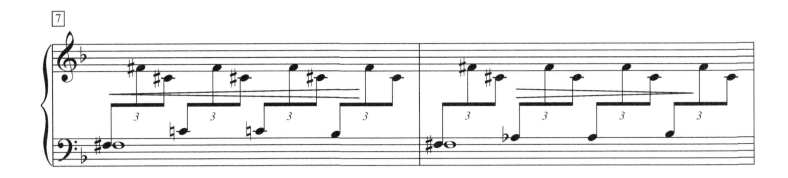

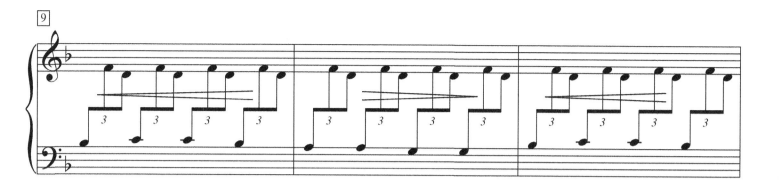

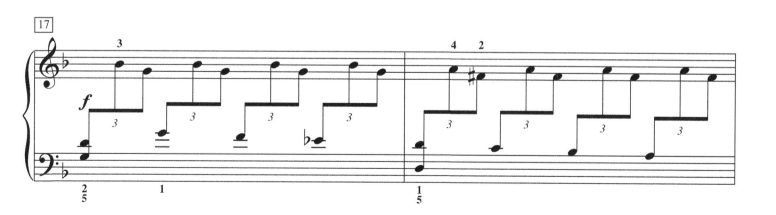

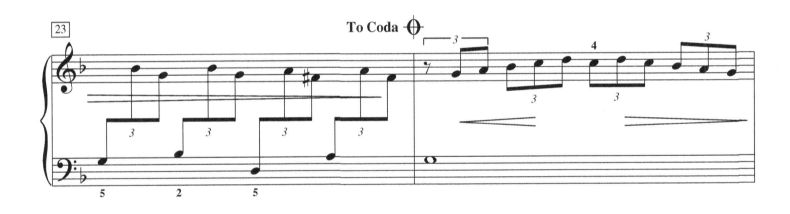

To Coda

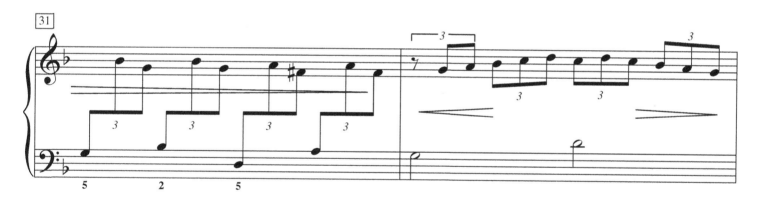

D.C. al Coda

ritardando

CODA

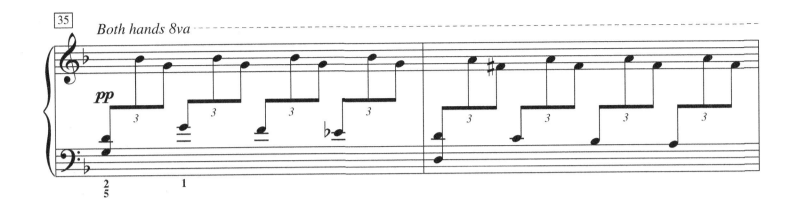

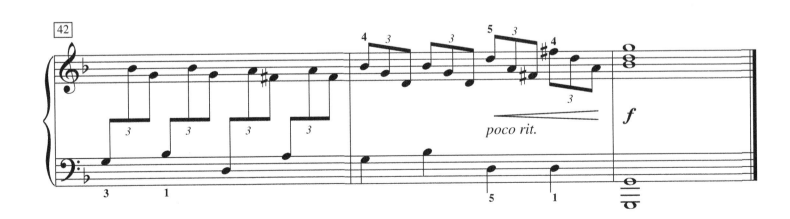

COMPOSER SHOWCASE
HAL LEONARD STUDENT PIANO LIBRARY

This series showcases great original piano music from our **Hal Leonard Student Piano Library** family of composers. Carefully graded for easy selection.

BILL BOYD

JAZZ BITS (AND PIECES)
Early Intermediate Level
00290312 11 Solos $7.99

JAZZ DELIGHTS
Intermediate Level
00240435 11 Solos $8.99

JAZZ FEST
Intermediate Level
00240436 10 Solos $8.99

JAZZ PRELIMS
Early Elementary Level
00290032 12 Solos $7.99

JAZZ SKETCHES
Intermediate Level
00220001 8 Solos $8.99

JAZZ STARTERS
Elementary Level
00290425 10 Solos $8.99

JAZZ STARTERS II
Late Elementary Level
00290434 11 Solos $7.99

JAZZ STARTERS III
Late Elementary Level
00290465 12 Solos $8.99

THINK JAZZ!
Early Intermediate Level
00290417 Method Book $12.99

TONY CARAMIA

JAZZ MOODS
Intermediate Level
00296728 8 Solos $6.95

SUITE DREAMS
Intermediate Level
00296775 4 Solos $6.99

SONDRA CLARK

DAKOTA DAYS
Intermediate Level
00296521 5 Solos $6.95

FLORIDA FANTASY SUITE
Intermediate Level
00296766 3 Duets $7.95

THREE ODD METERS
Intermediate Level
00296472 3 Duets $6.95

MATTHEW EDWARDS

**CONCERTO FOR
YOUNG PIANISTS**
FOR 2 PIANOS, FOUR HANDS
Intermediate Level Book/CD
00296356 3 Movements $19.99

CONCERTO NO. 2 IN G MAJOR
FOR 2 PIANOS, 4 HANDS
Intermediate Level Book/CD
00296670 3 Movements $17.99

PHILLIP KEVEREN

MOUSE ON A MIRROR
Late Elementary Level
00296361 5 Solos $8.99

MUSICAL MOODS
Elementary/Late Elementary Level
00296714 7 Solos $6.99

SHIFTY-EYED BLUES
Late Elementary Level
00296374 5 Solos $7.99

CAROL KLOSE

THE BEST OF CAROL KLOSE
Early to Late Intermediate Level
00146151 15 Solos $12.99

CORAL REEF SUITE
Late Elementary Level
00296354 7 Solos $7.50

DESERT SUITE
Intermediate Level
00296667 6 Solos $7.99

FANCIFUL WALTZES
Early Intermediate Level
00296473 5 Solos $7.95

GARDEN TREASURES
Late Intermediate Level
00296787 5 Solos $8.50

ROMANTIC EXPRESSIONS
Intermediate to Late Intermediate Level
00296923 5 Solos $8.99

WATERCOLOR MINIATURES
Early Intermediate Level
00296848 7 Solos $7.99

JENNIFER LINN

AMERICAN IMPRESSIONS
Intermediate Level
00296471 6 Solos $8.99

ANIMALS HAVE FEELINGS TOO
Early Elementary/Elementary Level
00147789 8 Solos $8.99

AU CHOCOLAT
Late Elementary/Early Intermediate Level
00298110 7 Solos $8.99

CHRISTMAS IMPRESSIONS
Intermediate Level
00296706 8 Solos $8.99

JUST PINK
Elementary Level
00296722 9 Solos $8.99

LES PETITES IMAGES
Late Elementary Level
00296664 7 Solos $8.99

LES PETITES IMPRESSIONS
Intermediate Level
00296355 6 Solos $8.99

REFLECTIONS
Late Intermediate Level
00296843 5 Solos $8.99

TALES OF MYSTERY
Intermediate Level
00296769 6 Solos $8.99

LYNDA LYBECK-ROBINSON

ALASKA SKETCHES
Early Intermediate Level
00119637 8 Solos $8.99

AN AWESOME ADVENTURE
Late Elementary Level
00137563 8 Solos $7.99

FOR THE BIRDS
Early Intermediate/Intermediate Level
00237078 9 Solos $8.99

WHISPERING WOODS
Late Elementary Level
00275905 9 Solos $8.99

MONA REJINO

CIRCUS SUITE
Late Elementary Level
00296665 5 Solos $8.99

COLOR WHEEL
Early Intermediate Level
00201951 6 Solos $9.99

IMPRESIONES DE ESPAÑA
Intermediate Level
00337520 6 Solos $8.99

IMPRESSIONS OF NEW YORK
Intermediate Level
00364212 .... $8.99

JUST FOR KIDS
Elementary Level
00296840 8 Solos $7.99

MERRY CHRISTMAS MEDLEYS
Intermediate Level
00296799 5 Solos $8.99

MINIATURES IN STYLE
Intermediate Level
00148088 6 Solos $8.99

PORTRAITS IN STYLE
Early Intermediate Level
00296507 6 Solos $8.99

EUGÉNIE ROCHEROLLE

CELEBRATION SUITE
Intermediate Level
00152724 3 Duets $8.99

**ENCANTOS ESPAÑOLES
(SPANISH DELIGHTS)**
Intermediate Level
00125451 6 Solos $8.99

JAMBALAYA
Intermediate Level
00296654 2 Pianos, 8 Hands $12.99
00296725 2 Pianos, 4 Hands $7.95

JEROME KERN CLASSICS
Intermediate Level
00296577 10 Solos $12.99

LITTLE BLUES CONCERTO
Early Intermediate Level
00142801 2 Pianos, 4 Hands $12.99

TOUR FOR TWO
Late Elementary Level
00296832 6 Duets $9.99

TREASURES
Late Elementary/Early Intermediate Level
00296924 7 Solos $8.99

JEREMY SISKIND

BIG APPLE JAZZ
Intermediate Level
00278209 8 Solos $8.99

MYTHS AND MONSTERS
Late Elementary/Early Intermediate Level
00148148 9 Solos $8.99

CHRISTOS TSITSAROS

**DANCES FROM AROUND
THE WORLD**
Early Intermediate Level
00296688 7 Solos $8.99

FIVE SUMMER PIECES
Late Intermediate/Advanced Level
00361235 5 Solos $12.99

LYRIC BALLADS
Intermediate/Late Intermediate Level
00102404 6 Solos $8.99

POETIC MOMENTS
Intermediate Level
00296403 8 Solos $8.99

SEA DIARY
Early Intermediate Level
00253486 9 Solos $8.99

SONATINA HUMORESQUE
Late Intermediate Level
00296772 3 Movements $6.99

SONGS WITHOUT WORDS
Intermediate Level
00296506 9 Solos $9.99

THREE PRELUDES
Early Advanced Level
00130747 3 Solos $8.99

THROUGHOUT THE YEAR
Late Elementary Level
00296723 12 Duets $6.95

ADDITIONAL COLLECTIONS

AT THE LAKE
by Elvina Pearce
Elementary/Late Elementary Level
00131642 10 Solos and Duets $7.99

CHRISTMAS FOR TWO
by Dan Fox
Early Intermediate Level
00290069 13 Duets $8.99

CHRISTMAS JAZZ
by Mike Springer
Intermediate Level
00296525 6 Solos $8.99

COUNTY RAGTIME FESTIVAL
by Fred Kern
Intermediate Level
00296882 7 Solos $7.99

LITTLE JAZZERS
by Jennifer Watts
Elementary/Late Elementary Level
00154573 9 Solos $8.99

PLAY THE BLUES!
by Luann Carman
Early Intermediate Level
00296357 10 Solos $9.99

ROLLER COASTERS & RIDES
by Jennifer & Mike Watts
Intermediate Level
00131144 8 Duets $8.99

HAL•LEONARD®
www.halleonard.com

Prices, contents, and availability subject to change without notice.

0321
144

Piano Recital Showcase

"What should my students play for the recital?" This series provides easy answers to this common question. For these winning collections, we've carefully selected some of the most popular and effective pieces from the **Hal Leonard Student Library** – from early-elementary to late-intermediate levels. You'll love the variety of musical styles found in each book.

PIANO RECITAL SHOWCASE PRE-STAFF
Pre-Staff Early Elementary Level
8 solos: Bumper Cars • Cherokee Lullaby • Fire Dance • The Hungry Spider • On a Magic Carpet • One, Two, Three • Pickled Pepper Polka • Pumpkin Song.
00296784 ....$7.99

BOOK 1
Elementary Level
12 solos: B.B.'s Boogie • In My Dreams • Japanese Garden • Jazz Jig • Joyful Bells • Lost Treasure • Monster March • Ocean Breezes • Party Cat Parade • Rainy Day Play • Sledding Fun • Veggie Song.
00296749 ....$8.99

BOOK 2
Late-Elementary Level
12 solos: Angelfish Arabesque • The Brontosaurus Bop • From the Land of Make-Believe • Ghosts of a Sunken Pirate Ship • The Happy Walrus • Harvest Dance • Hummingbird (L'oiseau-mouche) • Little Bird • Quick Spin in a Fast Car • Shifty-Eyed Blues • The Snake Charmer • Soft Shoe Shuffle.
00296748 ....$8.99

BOOK 3
Intermediate Level
10 solos: Castilian Dreamer • Dreaming Song • Jump Around Rag • Little Mazurka • Meaghan's Melody • Mountain Splendor • Seaside Stride • Snap to It! • Too Cool to Fool • Wizard's Wish.
00296747 ....$8.99

BOOK 4
Late-Intermediate Level
8 solos: Berceuse for Janey • Cafe Waltz • Forever in My Heart • Indigo Bay • Salsa Picante • Sassy Samba • Skater's Dream • Twilight on the Lake.
00296746 ....$8.99

CHRISTMAS EVE SOLOS
Intermediate Level
Composed for the intermediate level student, these pieces provide fresh and substantial repertoire for students not quite ready for advanced piano literature. Includes: Auld Lang Syne • Bring a Torch, Jeannette, Isabella • Coventry Carol • O Little Town of Bethlehem • Silent Night • We Wish You a Merry Christmas • and more.
00296877...$8.99

DUET FAVORITES
Intermediate Level
Five original duets for one piano, four hands from top composers Phillip Keveren, Eugénie Rocherolle, Sondra Clark and Wendy Stevens. Includes: Angel Falls • Crescent City Connection • Prime Time • A Wind of Promise • Yearning.
00296898...$9.99

FESTIVAL FAVORITES, BOOK 1
10 OUTSTANDING NFMC SELECTED SOLOS
Late Elementary/Early Intermediate Level
Proven piano solos fill this compilation of selected gems chosen for various National Federation of Music Clubs (NFMC) Junior Festival lists. Titles: Candlelight Prelude • Crazy Man's Blues • I've Gotta Toccata • Pagoda Bells • Tarantella • Toccata Festivo • Tonnerre sur les plaines (Thunder on the Plains) • Twister • Way Cool! • Wild Robot.
00118198...$10.99

FESTIVAL FAVORITES, BOOK 2
10 OUTSTANDING NFMC SELECTED SOLOS
Intermediate/Late Intermediate Level
Book 2 features: Barcarolle Impromptu • Cathedral Echoes (Harp Song) • Dance of the Trolls • Jasmine in the Mist • Jesters • Maestro, There's a Fly in My Waltz • Mother Earth, Sister Moon • Northwoods Toccata • Sounds of the Rain • Un phare dans le brouillard (A Lighthouse in the Fog).
00118202...$10.99

FESTIVAL GEMS – BOOK 1
Elementary/Late Elementary Level
This convenient collection features 10 NFMC-selected piano solos: Brooklyn's Waltz • Chimichanga Cha-Cha • Feelin' Happy • Footprints in the Snow • Lazy Daisy • New Orleans Jamboree • PBJ Blues • Pepperoni Pizza • Sneakin' Cake • Things That Go Bump in the Night. (Note: Solos are from previous NFMC lists.)
00193548 ....$10.99

HAL•LEONARD®
Visit our website at
www.halleonard.com/hlspl
for all the newest titles in this series and other books in the Hal Leonard Student Piano Library.

FESTIVAL GEMS – BOOK 2
Early Intermediate/Intermediate Level
Book 2 includes: Caravan • Chatterbox • In the Groove • Jubilation! • Kokopelli (Invention in Phrygian Mode) • La marée de soir (Evening Tide) • Reverie • Time Travel • Voiliers dans le vent (Sailboats in the Wind) • Williwaw.
00193587 ....$10.99

FESTIVAL GEMS – BOOK 3
Late Intermediate/Early Advanced Level
8 more NFMC-selected piano solos, including: Cuentos Del Matador (Tales of the Matador) • Daffodil Caprice • Love Song in the Rain • Midnight Prayer • Nocturne d'Esprit • Rapsodie • Scherzo • Urban Heartbeat.
00193588 ....$10.99

RAGTIME!
Early Intermediate/Intermediate Level
8 original rags from Bill Boyd, Phillip Keveren, Carol Klose, Jennifer Linn, Mona Rejino, Christos Tsitsaros and Jennifer & Mike Watts are featured in this solo piano collection. Includes: Butterfly Rag • Carnival Rag • Jump Around Rag • Nashville Rag • Ragtime Blue • St. Louis Rag • Swingin' Rag • Techno Rag.
00124242 ....$9.99

ROMANTIC INSPIRATIONS
Early Advanced Level
From "Arabesque" to "Nocturne" to "Rapsodie," the inspired pieces in this collection are a perfect choice for students who want to play beautiful, expressive and impressive literature at the recital. Includes: Arabesque • Journey's End • Nocturne • Nocturne d'Esprit • Prelude No. 1 • Rapsodie • Rondo Capriccioso • Valse d'Automne.
00296813...$8.99

SUMMERTIME FUN
Elementary Level
Twelve terrific originals from favorite HLSPL composers, all at the elementary level. Songs: Accidental Wizard • Butterflies and Rainbows • Chill Out! • Down by the Lake • The Enchanted Mermaid • Gone Fishin' • The Merry Merry-Go-Round • Missing You • Pink Lemonade • Rockin' the Boat • Teeter-Totter • Wind Chimes.
00296831 ....$7.99

Prices, content, and availability subject to change without notice.